The Best Birthday Mole Ever Had

Written by Fay Robinson ✹ Illustrated by Normand Chartier

"My birthday is coming up.
I think I'll plan a party," said Mole.

Mole made a card.

He sent the card to all his friends.

On the day of the party,
Mole baked a cake.
Then he cleaned his home.

Ladybug came first.
"Happy Birthday, Mole!" she said.
"This is for you." Ladybug gave Mole a huge card.

"Thank you very much," said Mole.

Snake came next.

"Happy Birthday, Mole!" he said.

"This is for you." Snake gave Mole ten flowers.

"Thank you very much," said Mole.

Rabbit came next.

"Happy Birthday, Mole!" he said.

"This is for you." Rabbit gave Mole a bag.

"Thank you very much," said Mole.

Mr. and Mrs. Fox came next.
"Happy Birthday, Mole!" they said.
"These are for you." Mr. and Mrs. Fox gave Mole two boxes.

"Thank you very much," said Mole.

Mule came next.
"Happy Birthday, Mole!" he said.
Mule pressed his nose into the open door. But — CRUNCH! — it didn't fit.

10

"Eeek!" said Ladybug.

"Oh, no!" said Snake.

"Yikes!" said Rabbit.

"Uh-oh!" said Mr. and Mrs. Fox.

"My home isn't big enough for a ladybug,
a snake, a rabbit, two foxes, a mule, and me.
My home isn't big enough for a party!" cried Mole.

"Don't cry," said Snake.

"We've had a nice time," said Mr. and Mrs. Fox.

"We can have the party outside!" said Mule.

"Yes! Let's go!" they all said as they dashed out the door.

Everyone had a great time.
It was the best birthday Mole ever had.